# Creaky Limericks

Written and illustrated by Hermione Ainley

Published by Colley Books, 11 Laud's Road.

Crick, Northamptonshire, NN6 7TJ

I know I'm a dozy old bat,

There can't be much doubt about that.

But things could be worse

Than just losing my purse

And my keys and my gloves and my hat.

This aging is no fun at all;

If I don't use the zimmer I fall.

And I'd like to make passes

But without my glasses

I can't see the lasses at all.

They say I've put on too much weight;

It must have been something I ate.

But I don't see how

I can lose it all now,

I've left it a little bit late.

If I could remember your name,

Or had some idea why you came

To mindlessly chat

About this and that,

I suspect I'd be bored just the same.

My problems are principally muscular,

Along with the cancer - testicular -

And dementia - senile -

And dysfunction - penile -

But nothing much else in particular.

I'm having a definite hunch

That my marriage has come to a crunch.

My dear lady wife

Says she took me for life,

Which in her view does not include lunch.

There's a picture of me in Australia,

Decked out in my finest regalia,

Looking delighted

While I'm being knighted;

So how come I feel such a failure?

I slip getting out of the bath,

And I trip when I walk up the path.

What worries me now

Is specifically how

I avoid tipping into the hearth?

Though I suffer from memory loss,

Quite frankly I don't give a toss.

No way am I fretting

About the forgetting,

But everything else makes me cross.

I feel that I really should mention,

Lest there be some misapprehension:

You need a good stash

Of your hard-fought-for cash

In a well-managed index-linked pension.

These days when I start to feel frisky

I know what I want would be risky,

So I just ask the nurse

If she'll kindly disburse

An extra-large measure of whisky.

No really! A touch of angina!

I honestly couldn't feel finer!

A little bit stiff -

It'll pass in a jiff -

I swear all my ailments are minor!

When I walked down the street men

would whistle;

I'd turn up my nose and I'd bristle.

But they don't whistle now

At a scraggy old cow

Who's a bag of old bones and some

gristle.

Alcohol's not an addiction -

Well perhaps just a minor affliction -

I feel when I drink

That it helps me to think,

But possibly that's all just fiction.

Christmas is no time for shocks.

You know when you open the box

There'll be no surprise,

Just a couple of ties,

Handkerchiefs, braces and socks.

I refuse to ask anyone's pardon

For failing to work in the garden.

I'd much rather stand

With a glass in my hand

Feeling my arteries harden.

POLLING STATION →

There's something I have to confess;

It's causing me dreadful distress.

When I lost my specs it

Meant I voted Brexit

And helped get us into this mess!

Although I am long in the tooth,

I seem to recall in my youth

That a four-letter word

Was like 'lady' or 'bird'

Whereas now it is something uncouth.

Do-gooders are tricky to spot;

If you don't pay attention a lot,

They'll take hold of your arm

To protect you from harm,

Whether you like it or not.

Why should I make any apology

For failing to master technology?

I'd much rather look

At a really good book

On the wonders of palaeontology.

# The End